COMMON CORE WRITING

Narrative Writing

Grade 3 Workbook

100 Guided Creative Writing Exercises and Prompts

ISBN 978-1494309589

CONTENTS

INTRODUCTION
For Parents, Teachers, and Tutors

This workbook will develop the narrative writing skills described in the Common Core State Standards. The standards state that to meet the goals, "students must devote significant time and effort to writing and producing numerous pieces over short and extended time frames throughout the year." This workbook provides this ongoing practice, while being specifically focused on developing the skills listed in the standards.

By completing the writing tasks in this book, students will be able to respond effectively to all types of writing tasks, while developing an understanding of the key features of narrative writing and gaining experience creating stories in many common genres.

Common Core State Standards

The Common Core State Standards are a set of standards that have been adopted by most American states. They describe what students are expected to be able to do. The standards divide writing skills based on text type and purpose. The three types of writing are opinion pieces, informative/explanatory texts, and narrative writing. This book focuses on narrative writing and has been specifically created to develop the skills listed in the Common Core State Standards. The full text of the narrative writing standard is included in the back of the book.

Developing Writing Skills

The first section of the book contains twelve sets of five writing prompts. Each set is focused on one key element of narrative writing. The first task in each set introduces the skill and guides students through the task. Students then master the skill by completing the four additional writing tasks. Many of the sets also include a warm-up exercise to prepare students for the set, to introduce and develop a key skill needed to complete the task well, or to help students focus on a key characteristic of narrative writing.

Applying Writing Skills

The second section of the book contains ten sets of four writing prompts. Each set is focused on one style or one genre of narrative writing. Students will use the key elements of narrative writing and apply the skills they have learned. Hints and tips are also included throughout the section to guide students. As well as developing general writing skills, this section will prepare students for the types of writing tasks found on assessment tasks and tests.

The Importance of Planning

The ability to plan writing is a key skill that leads to a strong performance on assessment tasks and tests. Effective planning produces writing that is focused, well-developed, well-organized, and complete. All the writing prompts in this book include a guided planning process that will teach students how to plan their work.

Developing Writing Skills

The exercises in this section will develop the writing skills needed to produce all types of narrative writing. Each set focuses on developing one specific skill.

Follow the instructions for each writing prompt. In some cases, you will write your work in the space provided. In other cases, you will write your work on a separate sheet of paper, or type your work.

Set 1: Describing Events in Order

Stories describe a set of events. Most stories describe the events in order. The beginning of a story describes what happens first. The middle of a story describes what happens next. The ending of a story describes what happens last. The three parts fit together to tell a whole story. Now read the story below.

When I first met Sandy, I thought she was boring. All she ever seemed to do was read books.

Then I became her partner in science class. I learned that she knows about all sorts of topics. She is always fun to talk to because she always has something new to tell me.

Now, Sandy and I are great friends. We have long chats about all sorts of interesting things.

The diagram below shows how the story is divided into three parts.

> **BEGINNING: DESCRIBE HOW THE NARRATOR FEELS AT FIRST**
>
> *The narrator thinks Sandy is boring.*

> **MIDDLE: DESCRIBE WHAT HAPPENS TO CHANGE HOW THE NARRATOR FEELS**
>
> *The narrator learns that Sandy knows lots of things.*

> **ENDING: DESCRIBE HOW THINGS HAVE CHANGED**
>
> *The narrator and Sandy are friends.*

The stories you write in this book will be divided into a beginning, a middle, and an ending.

Now practice describing events in order by completing the exercises.

Writing Prompt 1

Imagine that you are entering a talent contest. You think it will be easy to win. Then something happens to change how you feel. Complete the diagram below to show the events in order.

BEGINNING: DESCRIBE HOW YOU FEEL AT FIRST

I think winning the talent contest will be easy.

MIDDLE: DESCRIBE WHAT HAPPENS TO CHANGE HOW YOU FEEL

ENDING: DESCRIBE HOW THINGS HAVE CHANGED

Use the diagram above to write a few paragraphs describing the events in order.

_____

_____

_____

_____

_____

_____

_____

Writing Prompt 2

Imagine that you and a friend are riding a bike through the park. Then something goes wrong. Complete the diagram below to show the events in order.

BEGINNING: DESCRIBE WHAT YOU ARE DOING AT FIRST

I was riding slowly through the park.

MIDDLE: DESCRIBE WHAT GOES WRONG

ENDING: DESCRIBE WHAT YOU DO ABOUT WHAT GOES WRONG

Use the diagram above to write a few paragraphs describing the events in order.

_____

_____

_____

_____

_____

_____

_____

Writing Prompt 3

Imagine you order your usual lunch of a hamburger at a diner. Then the waiter brings you a very unusual meal. Complete the diagram below to show the events in order.

> **BEGINNING: DESCRIBE WHAT YOU ARE DOING AT FIRST**
>
> *I ordered a hamburger just like I always do.*

↓

> **MIDDLE: DESCRIBE HOW YOU ARE GIVEN A VERY UNUSUAL MEAL**

↓

> **ENDING: DESCRIBE WHAT YOU DO ABOUT THE MEAL YOU ARE GIVEN**

Use the diagram above to write a few paragraphs describing the events in order.

_____

_____

_____

_____

_____

_____

Writing Prompt 4

Imagine you are putting your running shoes on in the morning. Then you find an animal in one of your shoes. Complete the diagram below to show the events in order.

> **BEGINNING: DESCRIBE WHAT YOU ARE DOING AT FIRST**

↓

> **MIDDLE: DESCRIBE HOW YOU FIND AN ANIMAL IN ONE OF YOUR SHOES**

↓

> **ENDING: DESCRIBE WHAT YOU DO ABOUT FINDING THE ANIMAL**

Use the diagram above to write a few paragraphs describing the events in order.

_____

_____

_____

_____

_____

_____

Writing Prompt 5

Imagine you are brushing your teeth. Then you realize you have put something other than toothpaste on your toothbrush. Complete the diagram below to show the events in order.

```
┌─────────────────────────────────────────────────────────────────┐
│         BEGINNING: DESCRIBE WHAT YOU ARE DOING AT FIRST           │
│                                                                   │
│                                                                   │
└─────────────────────────────────────────────────────────────────┘
                                  ↓
┌─────────────────────────────────────────────────────────────────┐
│   MIDDLE: DESCRIBE HOW YOU REALIZE YOU ARE NOT BRUSHING WITH      │
│                         TOOTHPASTE                                │
│                                                                   │
└─────────────────────────────────────────────────────────────────┘
                                  ↓
┌─────────────────────────────────────────────────────────────────┐
│   ENDING: DESCRIBE WHAT YOU DO ABOUT NOT BRUSHING WITH TOOTHPASTE │
│                                                                   │
│                                                                   │
└─────────────────────────────────────────────────────────────────┘
```

Use the diagram above to write a few paragraphs describing the events in order.

_____

_____

_____

_____

_____

_____

_____

Warm-Up Exercise: Relating Events to Each Other

In the next set, you will learn about the plots of stories. A story's plot is the set of events that occur. These events are related to each other. Each diagram below shows the three events of a story. Finish each plot by completing the empty box with an event that makes sense. Focus on what could cause the last event.

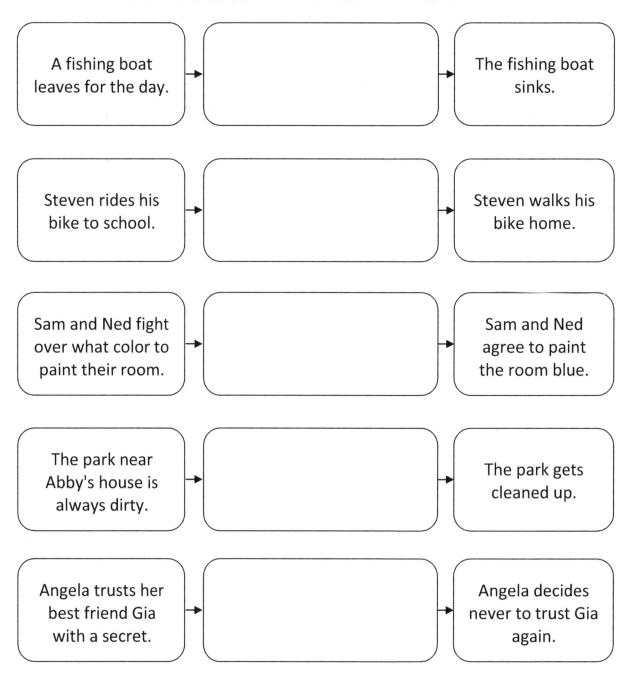

A fishing boat leaves for the day.		The fishing boat sinks.
Steven rides his bike to school.		Steven walks his bike home.
Sam and Ned fight over what color to paint their room.		Sam and Ned agree to paint the room blue.
The park near Abby's house is always dirty.		The park gets cleaned up.
Angela trusts her best friend Gia with a secret.		Angela decides never to trust Gia again.

Set 2: Understanding Plot

Writing Prompt 6

The plot of a story is what happens in a story. It is the sequence of events that occur in the story. Read the plot below.

Leo falls into the river. Odell saves Leo.

The sentences above describe the main events that occur in the story in order. First, Leo falls into the river. Then Odell tries to save Leo. Finally, Leo is saved.

The table below shows a story a student planned with this plot. The plan gives more details about what happened.

Use the plan below to write a story. Write or type a story of about 1 page.

The Beginning: Describe what happens first.   *Leo is playing next to the river. He slips and falls in. The fast-moving water washes him away.*   → **Start your story by writing a paragraph that describes these events.**
The Middle: Describe what happens next.   *Odell sees that Leo is in trouble. He grabs a long branch. He rushes farther down the river. He holds out the branch so Leo can grab it.*   → **Write two or three paragraphs that describe these events.**
The Ending: Describe what happens in the end.   *Leo grabs the branch. Odell pulls him in. Leo thanks his friend for saving him.*   → **End your story by writing a paragraph that describes these events.**

Writing Prompt 7

Write a story with the plot described below.

Sheena plays a mean trick on a friend. Sheena feels bad about it.

Start by thinking about the details of your story. Think about what trick Sheena plays. Think about what happens because of the trick and why Sheena feels bad.

Use the table below to plan your story. Write or type a story of about 1 page.

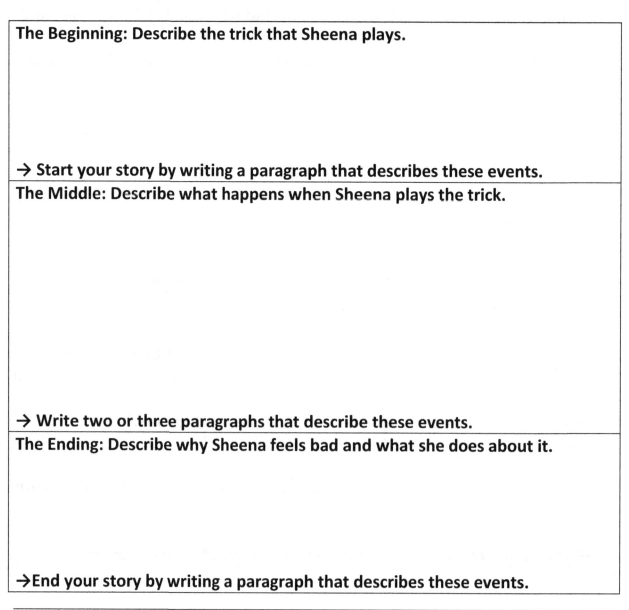

The Beginning: Describe the trick that Sheena plays.

→ **Start your story by writing a paragraph that describes these events.**

The Middle: Describe what happens when Sheena plays the trick.

→ **Write two or three paragraphs that describe these events.**

The Ending: Describe why Sheena feels bad and what she does about it.

→**End your story by writing a paragraph that describes these events.**

Writing Prompt 8

Write a story with the plot described below.

Callum lies and tells his friends he can play the guitar. Then he is asked to play for the class.

Use the table below to plan your story. Write or type a story of about 1 page.

The Beginning: Describe the lie that Callum tells.

→ **Start your story by writing a paragraph that describes these events.**

The Middle: Describe how the teacher asks Callum to play for the class.

→ **Write two or three paragraphs that describe these events.**

The Ending: Describe what Callum does when he is asked to play.

→**End your story by writing a paragraph that describes these events.**

Writing Prompt 9

Write a story with the plot described below.

Tony learns to ride a tractor, but he can't make the tractor stop.

Use the table below to plan your story. Write or type a story of about 1 page.

The Beginning: Describe how Tony learns that he cannot make the tractor stop.   **→ Start your story by writing a paragraph that describes these events.**
The Middle: Describe what happens as the tractor keeps going. You might describe some things that go wrong.   **→ Write two or three paragraphs that describe these events.**
The Ending: Describe what happens to make the tractor stop.   **→End your story by writing a paragraph that describes these events.**

Writing Prompt 10

Write a story with the plot described below.

Ming enters an art contest. She is surprised to win.

Use the table below to plan your story. Write or type a story of about 1 page.

The Beginning: Describe how Ming enters the art contest. You might describe the art that Ming enters and how she feels about entering the contest.   **→ Start your story by writing a paragraph that describes these events.**
The Middle: Describe how Ming learns that she has won.   **→ Write two or three paragraphs that describe these events.**
The Ending: Describe how Ming feels about winning.   **→End your story by writing a paragraph that shows how Ming feels.**

Warm-Up Exercise: Problems and Solutions

In the next set, you will learn how to write stories that describe how a problem is solved. There are often many ways that a problem could be solved. For each problem listed below, list three more ways the character could solve it.

1 Oliver is tired of walking his dog every afternoon.

He could make a dog-walking machine.

_____

_____

_____

2 Penny wants to learn to dance, but she has no money to take classes.

She could ask a friend who can dance to teach her.

_____

_____

_____

3 Robbie is bored one night after the power goes out.

He could start a game of hide-and-seek.

_____

_____

_____

Set 3: Using a Main Problem

Writing Prompt 11

Many stories are based around a main problem. The start of the story describes the main problem. The middle of the story describes how the character tries to solve the problem. The end of the story describes how the problem is solved. Read the problem below.

Dwayne thinks his friend is copying him on a test.

The sentence above describes the problem. There are many ways that Dwayne could try to solve this problem. The table below shows a story a student planned based on this problem.

Use the table below to plan your story. Write or type a story of about 1 page.

The Beginning: Describe the main problem.
Dwayne thinks his friend is copying him on a test.
→ **Start your story by writing a paragraph that introduces the problem.**
The Middle: Describe how Dwayne tries to solve the problem.
Dwayne starts writing wrong answers. He sees that his friend is copying those. Now he is sure his friend is copying him.
→ **Write two or three paragraphs that describe these events.**
The Ending: Describe what happens in the end to solve the problem.
Dwayne tells his friend to stop it. Dwayne's friend says sorry. Dwayne feels better.
→**End your story by writing a paragraph that shows that the problem is solved.**

Writing Prompt 12

Imagine that a character named Tyra does not have enough money to buy her brother a birthday present. Write a story that describes how Tyra solves the problem.

Use the table below to plan your story. Write or type a story of about 1 page.

The Beginning: Describe the main problem.

Tyra does not have enough money to buy her brother a birthday present.

→ **Start your story by writing a paragraph that introduces the problem.**

The Middle: Describe how Tyra tries to solve the problem.

→ **Write two or three paragraphs that describe these events.**

The Ending: Describe how the problem is solved.

→**End your story by writing a paragraph that shows that the problem is solved.**

Writing Prompt 13

Write a story based on the problem below.

A bear is too scared of the dark to go into its cave.

Use the table below to plan your story. Write or type a story of about 1 page.

The Beginning: Describe the main problem.   *A bear is too scared of the dark to go into its cave.*   **→ Start your story by writing a paragraph that introduces the problem.**
The Middle: Describe how the bear tries to solve the problem.   **→ Write two or three paragraphs that describe these events.**
The Ending: Describe how the problem is solved.   **→End your story by writing a paragraph that shows that the problem is solved.**

Writing Prompt 14

Write a story based on the problem below.

Marty forgets about a science project until the night before it is due.

Use the table below to plan your story. Write or type a story of about 1 page.

The Beginning: Describe the main problem.
Marty forgets about a science project until the night before it is due.
→ **Start your story by writing a paragraph that introduces the problem.**
The Middle: Describe how Marty tries to solve the problem.
→ **Write two or three paragraphs that describe these events.**
The Ending: Describe how the problem is solved.
→**End your story by writing a paragraph that shows that the problem is solved.**

Writing Prompt 15

Write a story based on the problem below.

Emi is sure her teacher is an alien, but nobody will believe her.

Use the table below to plan your story. Write or type a story of about 1 page.

The Beginning: Describe the main problem. *Emi is sure her teacher is an alien, but nobody will believe her.* → **Start your story by writing a paragraph that introduces the problem.**
The Middle: Describe how Emi tries to solve the problem.   → **Write two or three paragraphs that describe these events.**
The Ending: Describe how the problem is solved.   →**End your story by writing a paragraph that shows that the problem is solved.**

Warm-Up Exercise: Introducing the Setting

In the next set, you will learn how setting includes where a story takes place. When starting a story, you do not have to actually state the setting. Instead, you can include details that will show what the setting is.

For each setting listed below, write a sentence or two that would show what the setting is. The first one has been completed for you.

1 You are traveling in a car.

I put on my seatbelt and settled back in my seat. I was ready for the long drive ahead,

2 You are on an airplane.

_____

_____

3 You are in a shopping mall.

_____

_____

4 You are in a tree house.

_____

_____

Set 4: Understanding Setting

Writing Prompt 16

The setting of a story is where and when a story takes place. You will sometimes be asked to write a story with a given setting. Read the writing prompt below.

Write a story that takes place at a circus.

The writing prompt tells you where the events will take place. You have to decide what the events will be. Start by thinking about interesting things that could happen in the setting. You can also choose a main character. It could be someone in the circus or someone in the crowd. Here are some story ideas.

- Amy is a young girl in the crowd. She is scared when the clowns come out.
- It is the lion tamer's first night. He is worried about doing well.
- An elephant in the show runs straight out of the tent.

The table below shows a plan for a story about a circus elephant that runs away. Use the plan below to write a story. Write or type a story of about 1 page.

The Beginning: Introduce the setting and the main character.
Jo is at the circus. He is watching an elephant do a trick.
→ Start your story by writing a paragraph that describes where the main character is and what the main character is doing.
The Middle: Describe the interesting or exciting event that happens.
The elephant runs out of the tent. Everyone in the crowd starts looking for the elephant. Jo joins the search.
→ Write two or three paragraphs that describe these events.
The Ending: Describe what happens in the end.
Jo finds the elephant in the parking lot.
→End your story by writing a paragraph that describes these events.

Writing Prompt 17

Write a story that takes place in a cave. Start by thinking of three story ideas for a story set in a cave.

1. _____

2. _____

3. _____

Now choose the idea you want to base your story on. Use the table below to plan your story. Write or type a story of about 1 page.

The Beginning: Introduce the setting and the main character.   **→ Start your story by writing a paragraph that describes where the main character is and what the main character is doing.**
The Middle: Describe the interesting or exciting event that happens.   **→ Write two or three paragraphs that describe these events.**
The Ending: Describe what happens in the end.   **→End your story by writing a paragraph that describes these events.**

Writing Prompt 18

Write a story that takes place in the setting shown below.

Use the table below to plan your story. Write or type a story of about 1 page.

The Beginning: Introduce the setting and the main character.   **→ Start your story by writing a paragraph that describes where the main character is and what the main character is doing.**
The Middle: Describe the interesting or exciting event that happens.   **→ Write two or three paragraphs that describe these events.**
The Ending: Describe what happens in the end.   **→End your story by writing a paragraph that describes these events.**

Writing Prompt 19

Write a story that takes place in a museum at night.

Use the table below to plan your story. Write or type a story of about 1 page.

The Beginning: Introduce the setting and the main character.   **→ Start your story by writing a paragraph that describes where the main character is and what the main character is doing.**
The Middle: Describe the interesting or exciting event that happens.   **→ Write two or three paragraphs that describe these events.**
The Ending: Describe what happens in the end.   **→End your story by writing a paragraph that describes these events.**

Writing Prompt 20

Write a story that takes place on a raft traveling down a river.

Use the table below to plan your story. Write or type a story of about 1 page.

The Beginning: Introduce the setting and the main character.
→ Start your story by writing a paragraph that describes where the main character is and what the main character is doing.
The Middle: Describe the interesting or exciting event that happens.
→ Write two or three paragraphs that describe these events.
The Ending: Describe what happens in the end.
→End your story by writing a paragraph that describes these events.

Warm-Up Exercise: Characters and Traits

In the next set, you will learn about main characters. You will need to think about what characters are like. The qualities of a character are known as traits. You can show the traits by describing actions or by giving details. Complete the table below by adding an action or detail that shows each trait.

Trait	Action or Detail
messy	*always leaves dirty clothes on the floor*
funny	*was voted as the class clown*
bossy	
friendly	
lazy	
shy	
sneaky	
caring	
wise	

Set 5: Creating a Main Character

Writing Prompt 21

The main character of a story is who the story is mainly about. When writing a story, it is important to think about who the main character is and what the main character is like. Characters can be interesting because of their personalities. Read the description of the character Sammy below.

Sammy is a young girl who is rude to everybody.

Think about what might happen in a story about Sammy. What could happen because of Sammy's rudeness? How could Sammy learn not to be rude?

The table below shows a plan for a story about Sammy. Use the plan below to write a story. Write or type a story of about 1 page.

The Beginning: Introduce the main character. *Sammy is rude to everyone. A lot of people do not like her. She thinks that it doesn't matter what people think of her.* **→ Start your story by writing a paragraph that describes who the main character is and what the main character is like.**
The Middle: Describe what happens because of what the main character is like. *Sammy's teacher asks the students to work in groups. Nobody wants Sammy in their group. Sammy is upset.* **→ Write two or three paragraphs that describe these events.**
The Ending: Describe how the main character changes. *Sammy asks nicely if she can be part of a group. Everyone says yes. Sammy says thank you.* **→Write a paragraph that shows that the main character has changed.**

Writing Prompt 22

The characters in a story do not have to be people. Many stories have animals as characters. Write a story about a parrot that talks too much.

Use the table below to plan your story. Write or type a story of about 1 page.

The Beginning: Introduce the main character.   **→ Start your story by writing a paragraph that describes who the main character is and what the main character is like.**
The Middle: Describe what happens because of what the main character is like.   **→ Write two or three paragraphs that describe these events.**
The Ending: Describe how the main character changes.   **→Write a paragraph that shows that the main character has changed.**

Writing Prompt 23

Write a story about the character described below.

A baker gets too greedy.

Use the table below to plan your story. Write or type a story of about 1 page.

The Beginning: Introduce the main character.   **→ Start your story by writing a paragraph that describes who the main character is and what the main character is like.**
The Middle: Describe what happens because of what the main character is like.   **→ Write two or three paragraphs that describe these events.**
The Ending: Describe how the main character changes.   **→Write a paragraph that shows that the main character has changed.**

Writing Prompt 24

Many stories are based around a character who has a problem. Write a story about the character described below.

A postman keeps getting lost.

Use the table below to plan your story. Write or type a story of about 1 page.

The Beginning: Introduce the main character and the problem.
→ Start your story by writing a paragraph that describes who the main character is and what problem the main character has.
The Middle: Describe what happens because of the main character's problem.
→ Write two or three paragraphs that describe these events.
The Ending: Describe what happens in the end.
→End your story by writing a paragraph that describes these events.

Writing Prompt 25

Write a story about the character shown in the picture below. Think of a problem the character has.

Use the table below to plan your story. Write or type a story of about 1 page.

The Beginning: Introduce the main character and the problem.   **→ Start your story by writing a paragraph that describes who the main character is and what problem the main character has.**
The Middle: Describe what happens because of the main character's problem.   **→ Write two or three paragraphs that describe these events.**
The Ending: Describe what happens in the end.   **→End your story by writing a paragraph that describes these events.**

Warm-Up Exercise: Choosing Action Words

In the next set, you will learn about describing a character's actions. The words you use can help clearly show a character's actions by showing how a character is doing something. In the first example below, the word *chatted* is stronger because it shows that the talk was not serious. Now practice using strong words by replacing the underlined word in each sentence with a stronger one.

1   I talked to my friends about how much I liked the concert.

   I *chatted* to my friends about how much I liked the concert.

2   I put all my clothes into the suitcase and it just shut.

   I _____ all my clothes into the suitcase and it just shut.

3   I jumped onto the chair when I saw the mouse.

   I _____ onto the chair when I saw the mouse.

4   I hit the baseball and it flew out of the park.

   I _____ the baseball and it flew out of the park.

5   I smiled when I saw that my friends had baked me a cake.

   I _____ when I saw that my friends had baked me a cake.

6   I looked through the window to see if the bear was still there.

   I _____ through the window to see if the bear was still there.

Set 6: Describing Actions

A character's actions are what the character does. Actions tell readers a lot about a character. They can show what a character is doing, what a character is like, or what a character is thinking or feeling. Read the paragraph from a story below.

> Jane looked up at the clock again and then shook her head. It seemed like the hands had not moved at all. She looked back down at her textbook, but she couldn't think about math right now. She looked out the window and sighed.

The details in the paragraph suggest that Jane is in a classroom. The descriptions of Jane's actions give clues about what she is doing and how she feels. You can guess that she really wants the class to end because she is waiting for something. The table below shows the details given and what each detail suggests.

Sentence	What it Shows About Jane
Jane looked up at the clock again and then shook her head.	She is unhappy about what time it is.
It seemed like the hands had not moved at all.	She wants time to pass faster.
She looked back down at her textbook, but she couldn't think about math right now.	She has her mind on something else.
She looked out the window and sighed.	She is waiting for something. She feels annoyed with the time.

Now practice describing actions by completing the exercises.

Writing Prompt 26

Imagine that a character named Fiona is angry. List four actions that could be described to show how Fiona feels. The first one has been completed for you.

1. *Fiona slammed her hand down on the table.*

2. _____

_____

3. _____

_____

4. _____

_____

Write a paragraph that shows how Fiona feels and tells why she feels angry. You can use any of the actions above to help show how Fiona feels.

_____

_____

_____

_____

_____

_____

_____

Writing Prompt 27

Imagine that a character named Cooper is scared. List four actions that could be described to show how Cooper feels. The first one has been completed for you.

1. *Cooper pressed his hands together to stop them shaking.*

2. _____

_____

3. _____

_____

4. _____

_____

Write a paragraph that shows how Cooper feels and tells why he feels scared. You can use any of the actions above to help show how Cooper feels.

_____

_____

_____

_____

_____

_____

Writing Prompt 28

Imagine that a character named Manuel has to get up early, but is very tired. List four actions that could be described to show how Manuel feels.

1. *Manuel rolled over and put the pillow over his head.*

2. _____

_____

3. _____

_____

4. _____

_____

Write a paragraph that shows that Manuel does not want to get up because he is tired. You can use any of the actions above to help show how Manuel feels.

_____

_____

_____

_____

_____

_____

Writing Prompt 29

Imagine that a character named Hamid is running late. List four actions that could be described to show that Hamid is running late.

1. _____

_____

2. _____

_____

3. _____

_____

4. _____

_____

Write a paragraph that tells what Hamid is running late for. You can use any of the actions above to help show that Hamid is running late.

_____

_____

_____

_____

_____

_____

Writing Prompt 30

Imagine that a character named Aretha is lost. List four actions that could be described to show that Aretha is lost.

1. _____

   _____

2. _____

   _____

3. _____

   _____

4. _____

   _____

Write a paragraph that tells where Aretha is lost. You can use any of the actions above to help show that Aretha is lost.

_____

_____

_____

_____

_____

Warm-Up Exercise: Using Feelings in Stories

In the next set, you will use descriptions to show how characters feel. The feelings of characters are often important parts of stories. It is important to think about how characters would feel when events happen. Complete the table by adding a feeling to match each event or an event to match each feeling.

Event	Feeling
hearing a noise in the middle of the night	
being woken up early by a noisy bird	
getting a good score on a science project	
seeing it is sunny after a week of rain	
	bored
	excited
	embarrassed
	worried
	puzzled

Set 7: Using Descriptions to Show Feelings

Writing Prompt 31

Stories often need to show how characters feel. Good writers do not state how characters feel. They use descriptions to show how characters feel.

Read the first paragraph of a story on the next page. It describes what Jasmine does after coming second in a race. The paragraph does not state how Jasmine feels, but you can tell by her actions that she is upset.

The table below shows the plan for a story about Jasmine. Use the plan below to complete the story. Be sure to use descriptions to show how Jasmine feels during the story. Write your story on the next page.

The Beginning: Describe how the character feels at first.

Jasmine is upset when she comes second in a race. She wants to be happy for the winner, but she feels too sad.

→ This part has already been done for you. The first paragraph introduces the main character and shows how the main character feels.

The Middle: Describe what happens to change how the character feels.

The winner pats Jasmine on the back. She says that it was a close race. Jasmine starts thinking about the next race. She wonders if she can win it.

→ Write two or three paragraphs that describe these events.

The Ending: Describe how the character feels in the end.

Jasmine decides she is going to train harder. She decides that she can do better and win. She is excited about the next race.

→Write a paragraph that describes how the character feels now. You can use descriptions to show how the character feels.

Second Place

Jasmine stood near the finish line. She turned away from the rest of the runners. She stared down at the ground. She could hear the crowd cheering for the winner. She shook her head slowly and wiped away a tear.

_____

_____

_____

_____

_____

_____

_____

_____

_____

_____

_____

_____

_____

Writing Prompt 32

Write a story about the character described below. Use descriptions to show how the character feels.

Corey's basketball team is behind by one point. Corey really wants to win. Then Corey scores the winning basket.

Use the table below to plan your story. Write or type a story of about 1 page.

The Beginning: Describe how the character feels at first.   → **Start your story by writing a paragraph that introduces the main character and shows how the main character feels.**
The Middle: Describe what happens to change how the character feels.   → **Write two or three paragraphs that describe these events.**
The Ending: Describe how the character feels in the end.   → **Write a paragraph that describes how the character feels now. You can use descriptions to show how the character feels.**

Writing Prompt 33

Write a story about the character described below. Use descriptions to show how the character feels.

Anna learns that her friend Beth has been telling lies about her.

Use the table below to plan your story. Write or type a story of about 1 page.

The Beginning: Describe how the character feels at first.   **→ Start your story by writing a paragraph that introduces the main character and shows how the main character feels.**
The Middle: Describe what happens to change how the character feels.   **→ Write two or three paragraphs that describe these events.**
The Ending: Describe how the character feels in the end.   **→Write a paragraph that describes how the character feels now. You can use descriptions to show how the character feels.**

Writing Prompt 34

Write a story about the character described below. Use descriptions to show how the character feels.

Damien rock climbs down a steep cliff.

Use the table below to plan your story. Write or type a story of about 1 page.

The Beginning: Describe how the character feels at first.   → **Start your story by writing a paragraph that introduces the main character and shows how the main character feels.**
The Middle: Describe what happens to change how the character feels.   → **Write two or three paragraphs that describe these events.**
The Ending: Describe how the character feels in the end.   →**Write a paragraph that describes how the character feels now. You can use descriptions to show how the character feels.**

Writing Prompt 35

Write a story about the character described below. Use descriptions to show how the character feels.

Karen is afraid of speaking in front of crowds, but she wants to overcome her fear. Karen is going to give a speech to her class.

Use the table below to plan your story. Write or type a story of about 1 page.

The Beginning: Describe how the character feels at first.   **→ Start your story by writing a paragraph that introduces the main character and shows how the main character feels.**
The Middle: Describe what happens to change how the character feels.   **→ Write two or three paragraphs that describe these events.**
The Ending: Describe how the character feels in the end.   **→Write a paragraph that describes how the character feels now. You can use descriptions to show how the character feels.**

Warm-Up Exercise: Using Punctuation in Dialogue

In the next set, you will write stories that include dialogue. It is important to use the right punctuation when writing dialogue. Look at these examples.

"I am cold," Harry said.

"Where are we going?" I asked.

"Wait for me!" Jo called.

Anna said, "I am sure we will win."

"We should go home now," Troy said. "It is getting late."

Notice that there are quotation marks around the words spoken. Notice that commas, question marks, and exclamation points at the end of words spoken are placed inside the quotation marks. Now practice by adding the quotation marks to the sentences below.

1 George said, I am feeling sick today.

2 Is everything all right? Carol asked.

3 I liked the camp, Mark said. I would like to go again.

4 Watch out! Jenna yelled.

5 Sandy asked, Can I wash the dishes up later?

6 The party was great, Hannah said. Why didn't you come?

7 We should plan something fun to do on the weekend, Kyle said.

Set 8: Using Dialogue

Writing Prompt 36

Dialogue are words spoken by characters. Read the start of a story on the next page.

The words spoken by the characters show you what is happening in the story. You can tell that Morgan is having trouble with the math problems. You can guess that Morgan feels annoyed. You can tell that Jo wants to help. You can also guess that Jo is a nice person.

The table below shows a story a student planned that started with this dialogue. Use the plan below to write a story. Write your story on the next page.

The Beginning: Describe the main characters and the main problem.   *Morgan cannot do his math problems. He gets annoyed. Jo offers to help.*   **→ This part has already been done for you. The first paragraph tells who the story is about and what the main problem is.**
The Middle: Describe what happens next.   *Jo teaches Morgan how to do the problems.*   **→ Continue the story by telling what happens. You can use dialogue and descriptions to show what is happening or how characters feel.**
The Ending: Describe what happens in the end.   *Morgan is able to do the problems on his own. He is glad that his friend helped him.*   **→ End your story by telling what happens. You can use dialogue and descriptions to show what is happening or how characters feel.**

A Helping Hand

Morgan threw his pen down on his desk.
"I just cannot work out these math problems," Morgan sighed.
"It's easy," Jo replied. "I can help you with it."

_____

_____

_____

_____

_____

_____

_____

_____

_____

_____

_____

_____

_____

_____

Writing Prompt 37

Write a story that begins with the sentence below.

"We shouldn't be in here," Chan whispered.

Start by thinking about what could be happening in the story. Where could Chan be? What could he be doing? Why shouldn't he be there?

Use the table below to plan your story. Write or type a story of about 1 page.

The Beginning: Describe what happens first.   **→ Start your story by telling who the story is about and what is happening.**
The Middle: Describe what happens next.   **→ Continue the story by telling what happens. You can use dialogue and descriptions to show what is happening or how characters feel.**
The Ending: Describe what happens in the end.   **→ End your story by telling what happens. You can use dialogue and descriptions to show what is happening or how characters feel.**

Writing Prompt 38

Write a story that begins with the sentence below.

"Is that a goat in your backyard?" Emilia asked.

Use the table below to plan your story. Write or type a story of about 1 page.

The Beginning: Describe what happens first.
→ **Start your story by telling who the story is about and what is happening.**
The Middle: Describe what happens next.
→ **Continue the story by telling what happens. You can use dialogue and descriptions to show what is happening or how characters feel.**
The Ending: Describe what happens in the end.
→ **End your story by telling what happens. You can use dialogue and descriptions to show what is happening or how characters feel.**

Writing Prompt 39

Lacey clapped her hands. She had just heard some great news. She had never felt happier. Write a story about Lacey's good news. Use at least two lines of dialogue in your story.

Use the table below to plan your story. Write or type a story of about 1 page.

The Beginning: Describe what happens first.   → **Start your story by telling who the story is about and what is happening.**
The Middle: Describe what happens next.   → **Continue the story by telling what happens. You can use dialogue and descriptions to show what is happening or how characters feel.**
The Ending: Describe what happens in the end.   → **End your story by telling what happens. You can use dialogue and descriptions to show what is happening or how characters feel.**

Writing Prompt 40

Cedric suddenly realized that the school bus was not taking him to school. He looked at the bus driver. He had never seen him before. Write a story about Cedric's bus trip. Use at least two lines of dialogue in your story.

Use the table below to plan your story. Write or type a story of about 1 page.

The Beginning: Describe what happens first.   → **Start your story by telling who the story is about and what is happening.**
The Middle: Describe what happens next.   → **Continue the story by telling what happens. You can use dialogue and descriptions to show what is happening or how characters feel.**
The Ending: Describe what happens in the end.   → **End your story by telling what happens. You can use dialogue and descriptions to show what is happening or how characters feel.**

Set 9: Understanding Theme

Writing Prompt 41

The theme of a story is an important idea in the story. It is often a lesson that the story teaches, or a lesson a character learns. Read the theme below.

Do not try to do too many things at once.

Think about what could happen in a story to teach this lesson. Remember that the story does not have to state the lesson. Instead, readers learn the lesson by what happens in the story. Think about different ways that someone could try to do too many things at once.

The table below shows a story a student planned with this theme. Use the plan below to write a story. Write or type a story of about 1 page.

The Beginning: Introduce the main character and show what he or she is like.
Juan finds a web site where you can get pen pals. Juan decides he wants one pen pal from every single country.
→ Start by showing what the main character is like and what is happening.
The Middle: Describe what happens to teach the character a lesson.
Juan starts writing letters to pen pals. He writes to 50 different people in 50 different countries. He starts getting everyone confused. He starts getting tired of writing.
→ Write two or three paragraphs that describe these events.
The Ending: Describe how the character has learned a lesson.
Juan cannot keep up with his pen pals. He writes each one a final letter saying sorry. Then he chooses one pen pal.
→ Write a paragraph that shows how the character has changed.

Writing Prompt 42

Write a story with the message below.

Do not be afraid to ask for help.

Start by thinking of a story idea where a character should ask for help, but does not. Use the table below to plan your story. Write or type a story of about 1 page.

The Beginning: Describe who the main character is and why the main character should ask for help.   → **Write a paragraph telling who the story is about and what is happening.**
The Middle: Describe what happens because the character doesn't ask for help.   → **Write two or three paragraphs that describe these events.**
The Ending: Describe how the character finally asks for help.   → **Write a paragraph that shows how the character has changed.**

Writing Prompt 43

Write a story on the theme of friendship. Start by thinking about what you want to say about friendship. Add two more ideas to the list below.

1. *Friends are there for you when you need them.*

2. *It can be hard to make new friends, but it is worth it.*

3. _____

4. _____

Now choose the idea you want to base your story on. Use the table below to plan your story. Write or type a story of about 1 page.

The Beginning: Introduce the main character and show what he or she is like.   **→ Start by showing what the main character is like and what is happening.**
The Middle: Describe what happens to teach the character a lesson.   **→ Write two or three paragraphs that describe these events.**
The Ending: Describe how the character has learned a lesson.   **→ Write a paragraph that shows how the character has changed.**

Writing Prompt 44

Write a story on the theme of laziness. Start by thinking about what you want to say about laziness. List three ideas below.

1. _____

2. _____

3. _____

Now choose the idea you want to base your story on. Use the table below to plan your story. Write or type a story of about 1 page.

The Beginning: Introduce the main character and show what he or she is like.
→ **Start by showing what the main character is like and what is happening.**
The Middle: Describe what happens to teach the character a lesson.
→ **Write two or three paragraphs that describe these events.**
The Ending: Describe how the character has learned a lesson.
→ **Write a paragraph that shows how the character has changed.**

Writing Prompt 45

The title of a story sometimes tells what the message of the story is. Write a story with the title below.

Family Comes First

Start by thinking about what the message of the story is. Then think about what could happen in the story to communicate the message. Use the table below to plan your story. Write or type a story of about 1 page.

The Beginning: Introduce the main character and show what he or she is like.
→ Start by showing what the main character is like and what is happening.
The Middle: Describe what happens to teach the character a lesson.
→ Write two or three paragraphs that describe these events.
The Ending: Describe how the character has learned a lesson.
→ Write a paragraph that shows how the character has changed.

Warm-Up Exercise: Writing in First-Person

In the next set, you will write stories in first-person point of view. This means that you will write stories as if they are happening to you. You will use words like *I, me, my, mine, we,* and *our.*

The sentences below are all written in third-person point of view. Rewrite each sentence in first-person by changing the underlined words.

1 Ken walked into the room and took his seat.

I walked into the room and took my seat.

2 Joseph placed his bag on the ground.

_____

3 Justine was mad at her team because she knew they should have won.

_____

4 Jade saw that the last name on the list was hers.

_____

5 Craig was sad that nobody asked him how he was feeling.

_____

6 Justine asked her sister to help her clean their room.

_____

Set 10: Using a Narrator

Writing Prompt 46

Stories have different points of view. A story with a first-person point of view has a narrator telling the story. Narrators describe the events as if they are happening to them.

Read the first few sentences of a story on the next page. The narrator of the story is a person who is about to cross a river. One benefit of writing in first-person is that you can have narrators describe their feelings. In this story, you can describe how the narrator feels worried at the start. Then you can describe how the narrator feels thankful after crossing the river.

The table below shows the plan for a story about crossing the river. The plan is also written in first-person point of view. Use the plan below to complete the story. Write your story on the next page.

The Beginning: Describe what is happening and how the narrator feels.
I am about to cross the river. I feel worried about getting across the river safely.
→ This part has already been done for you. The first paragraph introduces the narrator and shows how the narrator feels.
The Middle: Describe what happens next.
I leap into the river and swim as fast as I can. I am carried downstream, but I make it across.
→ Write two or three paragraphs that describe these events.
The Ending: Describe what happens in the end and how the narrator feels.
I climb up onto the bank. I feel great about being safely on the other side.
→Write a paragraph that tells what happens in the end and shows how the narrator feels.

The Swim

I look at the rushing water. It is only a short swim across, but the water is moving fast. I know I will have to swim quickly. I tell myself that everything will be all right.

_____

_____

_____

_____

_____

_____

_____

_____

_____

_____

_____

_____

_____

Writing Prompt 47

Write a story that begins with the sentences on the next page.

Use the table below to plan your story. Write your story on the next page.

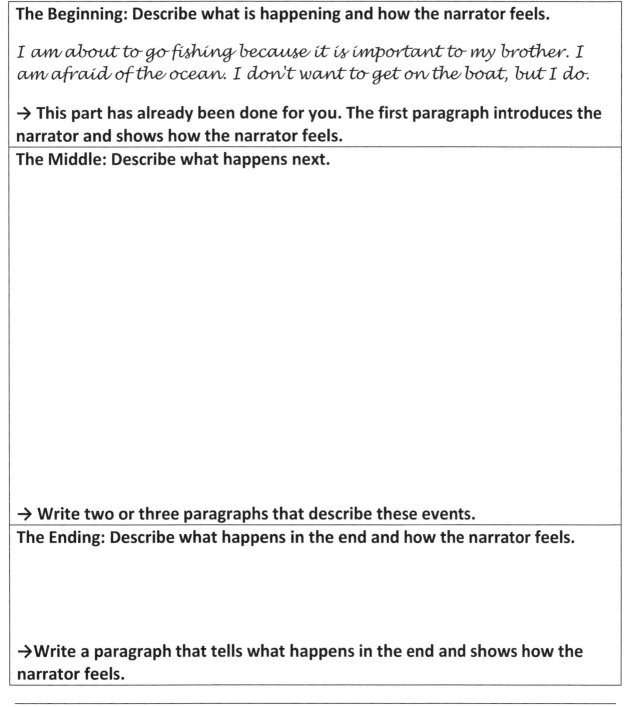

The Beginning: Describe what is happening and how the narrator feels.

I am about to go fishing because it is important to my brother. I am afraid of the ocean. I don't want to get on the boat, but I do.

→ This part has already been done for you. The first paragraph introduces the narrator and shows how the narrator feels.

The Middle: Describe what happens next.

→ Write two or three paragraphs that describe these events.

The Ending: Describe what happens in the end and how the narrator feels.

→Write a paragraph that tells what happens in the end and shows how the narrator feels.

_____

I have never liked the ocean. I feel like it could sweep me away anytime it chose to. But my brother's wish was for the family to go fishing. So I tried to put on a brave face as I boarded the tiny boat.

_____

_____

_____

_____

_____

_____

_____

_____

_____

_____

_____

_____

Writing Prompt 48

Write a story from the point of view of a farmer hoping that a wild storm will not ruin all his crops.

Use the table below to plan your story. Write or type a story of about 1 page.

The Beginning: Describe what is happening and how the narrator feels.
→ Start your story by writing a paragraph that introduces the narrator and shows how the narrator feels.
The Middle: Describe what happens next.
→ Write two or three paragraphs that describe these events.
The Ending: Describe what happens in the end and how the narrator feels.
→Write a paragraph that tells what happens in the end and shows how the narrator feels.

Writing Prompt 49

Write a story from the point of view of a girl who has just learned that her best friend is moving away.

Use the table below to plan your story. Write or type a story of about 1 page.

The Beginning: Describe what is happening and how the narrator feels.   **→ Start your story by writing a paragraph that introduces the narrator and shows how the narrator feels.**
The Middle: Describe what happens next.   **→ Write two or three paragraphs that describe these events.**
The Ending: Describe what happens in the end and how the narrator feels.   **→Write a paragraph that tells what happens in the end and shows how the narrator feels.**

Writing Prompt 50

Write a story from the point of view of a firefighter about to fight his first fire.

Use the table below to plan your story. Write or type a story of about 1 page.

The Beginning: Describe what is happening and how the narrator feels.
→ Start your story by writing a paragraph that introduces the narrator and shows how the narrator feels.
The Middle: Describe what happens next.
→ Write two or three paragraphs that describe these events.
The Ending: Describe what happens in the end and how the narrator feels.
→Write a paragraph that tells what happens in the end and shows how the narrator feels.

Warm-Up Exercise: Using Transition Words

In the next set, you will describe events in order. You will use words and phrases to tell when events occur, to show the order of events, or to show how much time has passed. The table below gives examples of words and phrases used for each purpose.

When Events Occur	Order of Events	How Much Time Passed
today	later	soon
yesterday	after	shortly
on Friday	next	after a short time
this morning	afterwards	the day after
in June	first	in just a few minutes
at noon	second	many hours later
late at night	before	later that week
around lunchtime	last	after a long wait

Choose two examples of each type. Write a sentence that includes each word or phrase you chose.

When Events Occur

1. _____

2. _____

Order of Events

1. _____

2. _____

How Much Time Passed

1. _____

2. _____

Set 11: Understanding Sequence

Writing Prompt 51

The events in most stories are described in sequence, or in the order that events happen. Read the start of a story on the next page.

The table below shows the plan for a story about Tia. Notice that the story begins at midnight and ends in the early morning. You can use transition words and phrases to move the story forward. These are words and phrases that tell when the events take place. For example, in the middle of the story you might describe how Tia lay awake "for hours" to show the time that passes. At the end of the story you might say that "the sun finally came up" to show that it is now morning.

Use the plan below to complete the story. Write your story on the next page. Remember to use transition words and phrases to tell when events take place.

The Beginning: Describe what happens first. *Tia is camping. It is just past midnight when she hears a scratching noise.* **→ This part has already been done for you. The first paragraph describes what happens first.**
The Middle: Describe what happens next. *Tia lies awake all night worrying about the sound.* **→ Write two or three paragraphs that describe these events.**
The Ending: Describe what happens in the end. *Tia feels safer once it begins to get light. She leaves the tent to see what the sound is. She sees the leaves of a tree are brushing against the tent.* **→ End your story by writing a paragraph that describes these events.**

The Longest Night

The sound of the scratching woke me. I lay in the darkness wondering what it could be. It was just past midnight and my friends in the tent were fast asleep.

_____

_____

_____

_____

_____

_____

_____

_____

_____

_____

_____

_____

Writing Prompt 52

Write a story that begins with the sentence below.

Just after sunset, we all met beneath the old clock tower.

Use the table below to plan your story. Write or type a story of about 1 page.

The Beginning: Describe what happens first.   **→ Start your story by telling who the story is about and what is happening.**
The Middle: Describe what happens next.   **→ Continue the story by telling what happens. You can use transition words and phrases to tell when events are happening.**
The Ending: Describe what happens in the end.   **→ End your story by telling what happens. You can use transition words and phrases to tell when events are happening.**

Writing Prompt 53

Write a story that begins with the sentence below.

As soon as class finished, I raced home as fast as I could.

Use the table below to plan your story. Write or type a story of about 1 page.

The Beginning: Describe what happens first.   **→ Start your story by telling who the story is about and what is happening.**
The Middle: Describe what happens next.   **→ Continue the story by telling what happens. You can use transition words and phrases to tell when events are happening.**
The Ending: Describe what happens in the end.   **→ End your story by telling what happens. You can use transition words and phrases to tell when events are happening.**

Writing Prompt 54

Write a story that includes the sentence below. You can use the sentence at the start, middle, or end of your story.

Suddenly, Oliver raced to the front of the bus.

Use the table below to plan your story. Write or type a story of about 1 page.

The Beginning: Describe what happens first.   **→ Start your story by telling who the story is about and what is happening.**
The Middle: Describe what happens next.   **→ Continue the story by telling what happens. You can use transition words and phrases to tell when events are happening.**
The Ending: Describe what happens in the end.   **→ End your story by telling what happens. You can use transition words and phrases to tell when events are happening.**

Writing Prompt 55

Write a story that includes the sentence below. You can use the sentence at the start, beginning, or end of your story.

As I heard the clock strike noon, I knew it was too late.

Use the table below to plan your story. Write or type a story of about 1 page.

The Beginning: Describe what happens first.   **→ Start your story by telling who the story is about and what is happening.**
The Middle: Describe what happens next.   **→ Continue the story by telling what happens. You can use transition words and phrases to tell when events are happening.**
The Ending: Describe what happens in the end.   **→ End your story by telling what happens. You can use transition words and phrases to tell when events are happening.**

Set 12: Using Humor

Writing Prompt 56

Humorous stories can describe a funny series of events. It is often funny when things go wrong. Now imagine that you are cooking something. Think about what could go wrong. You can make your story funnier by describing things that could not happen in real life. Maybe a cake could rise so much that it fills up the whole kitchen. Maybe a pot could boil over and cause a flood.

Use the table below to plan your story. Write or type a story of about 1 page.

The Beginning: Describe what you are cooking.
→ Start your story by writing a paragraph that tells what you are cooking. You might also tell why you are cooking it.
The Middle: Describe what goes wrong.
→ Continue the story by writing two or three paragraphs that show what goes wrong. You can use humor in this part.
The Ending: Describe what happens in the end.
→End your story by writing a paragraph that describes these events.

Writing Prompt 57

Imagine that the object below comes to life. Write a story about what happens.

Use the table below to plan your story. Write or type a story of about 1 page.

The Beginning: Describe how the object comes to life.
→ Start your story by writing a paragraph that tells how the object first comes to life.
The Middle: Describe what happens next.
→ Continue the story by writing two or three paragraphs that show what happens when the object comes to life. You can use humor in this part.
The Ending: Describe what happens in the end.
→End your story by writing a paragraph that describes these events.

Writing Prompt 58

Animals can be great characters for funny stories. Write a story based on the idea below.

A shy giraffe is tired of always standing out.

Use the table below to plan your story. Write or type a story of about 1 page.

The Beginning: Describe the giraffe's main problem.
→ Start your story by writing a paragraph that introduces the problem.
The Middle: Describe how the giraffe tries to solve the problem.
→ Write two or three paragraphs that describe these events. You can use humor in this part.
The Ending: Describe how the problem is solved.
→End your story by writing a paragraph that shows that the problem is solved.

Writing Prompt 59

Leah's sister never seemed to stop talking. Leah decided to teach her sister a lesson. Write a story about how Leah stops her sister from talking so much.

Use the table below to plan your story. Write or type a story of about 1 page.

The Beginning: Describe Leah's main problem.
→ Start your story by writing a paragraph that introduces the problem.
The Middle: Describe how Leah tries to solve the problem.
→ Write two or three paragraphs that describe these events. You can use humor in this part.
The Ending: Describe how the problem is solved.
→End your story by writing a paragraph that shows that the problem is solved.

Writing Prompt 60

Events from your own life can make humorous stories. Think of a funny event from your life. Write a story based on that event.

Use the table below to plan your story. Write or type a story of about 1 page.

The Beginning: Describe what happens first.
→ Start your story by telling who the story is about and what is happening.
The Middle: Describe what happens next.
→ Write two or three paragraphs that describe these events. You can use humor in this part.
The Ending: Describe what happens in the end.
→ End your story by writing a paragraph that describes these events.

Applying Writing Skills

The exercises in this section will provide practice writing different types of narrative texts. Each set focuses on one type of narrative writing.

Follow the instructions for each writing prompt, and plan your work in the space provided. Then write your work on a separate sheet of paper, or type your work.

After completing your work, review your writing. You can use the checklist on the next page to help you review your work.

Review Checklist

Organization

- ❏ Is there a beginning, a middle, and an ending?
- ❏ Is the beginning strong?
- ❏ Does the beginning introduce important details well?
- ❏ Is the middle well-organized?
- ❏ Do the events flow smoothly?
- ❏ Are words and phrases used to show event order?
- ❏ Is the ending strong?
- ❏ Does the ending tie up the story?

Content

- ❏ Are the actions of characters described well?
- ❏ Are descriptions used well?
- ❏ Are details used to describe things clearly?
- ❏ Are strong words used to help readers imagine the setting, the characters, or the events?

Grammar and Usage

- ❏ Are words spelled correctly?
- ❏ Is capitalization used correctly?
- ❏ Is punctuation used correctly?
- ❏ If dialogue is included, is it punctuated correctly?
- ❏ Are complete sentences used?
- ❏ Are sentences written correctly?
- ❏ Do the sentences make sense?
- ❏ Are words used correctly?

Set 13: Write from a Picture Prompt

Writing Prompt 61

Sometimes you will be asked to write a story based on a picture. Stories based on pictures should not just describe what the picture shows. Instead, you should think of an idea for a story based on the picture. Look at the picture below.

You can see that the family are having a picnic. Think about what could happen to make the story interesting. One idea is that a bird swoops down and steals the sandwiches. Write down some other ideas you have below.

Notes and Ideas

Now choose the story idea you want to use. Use the table below to plan your story. Write or type a story of 1 to 2 pages.

The Beginning: Describe what happens first.   **→ Start your story by telling who the story is about and what is happening.**
The Middle: Describe what happens next.   **→ Continue the story by writing two or three paragraphs that describe what happens.**
The Ending: Describe what happens in the end.   **→ End your story by writing a paragraph that describes these events.**

Writing Prompt 62

Look at the picture below. Write a story based on the picture.

You can use the people in the kayak as the main characters. Now think about what could happen to the people in the kayak. You can list some ideas or take notes below.

 This picture prompt could be used to write a funny story. Try thinking of something funny that could happen to the people in the kayak.

Notes and Ideas

Now choose the story idea you want to use. Use the table below to plan your story. Write or type a story of 1 to 2 pages.

The Beginning: Describe what happens first.
→ Start your story by telling who the story is about and what is happening.
The Middle: Describe what happens next.
→ Continue the story by writing two or three paragraphs that describe what happens.
The Ending: Describe what happens in the end.
→ End your story by writing a paragraph that describes these events.

Writing Prompt 63

Look at the picture below. Write a story based on the picture.

Think about who the two people are and what they are doing. You can list some ideas or take notes below.

 This picture prompt could be used to write a story about a girl who is scared of going sledding. The story could describe how she faces her fear.

Notes and Ideas

Now choose the story idea you want to use. Use the table below to plan your story. Write or type a story of 1 to 2 pages.

The Beginning: Describe what happens first.
→ Start your story by telling who the story is about and what is happening.
The Middle: Describe what happens next.
→ Continue the story by writing two or three paragraphs that describe what happens.
The Ending: Describe what happens in the end.
→ End your story by writing a paragraph that describes these events.

Writing Prompt 64

Look at the picture below. Write a story based on the picture.

You can use the girl shown as the main character. Now think about what could happen to the girl. You can list some ideas or take notes below.

 Try to think of something exciting or interesting that happens.

Notes and Ideas

Now choose the story idea you want to use. Use the table below to plan your story. Write or type a story of 1 to 2 pages.

The Beginning: Describe what happens first.
→ Start your story by telling who the story is about and what is happening.
The Middle: Describe what happens next.
→ Continue the story by writing two or three paragraphs that describe what happens.
The Ending: Describe what happens in the end.
→ End your story by writing a paragraph that describes these events.

Set 14: Write a Personal Narrative

Writing Prompt 65

A personal narrative is a story that is based on events in your own life. Personal narratives usually tell about one event in your life. Just like a normal story, your personal narrative should have a beginning, a middle, and an ending. Think of it as writing a story where you are the main character. Your story should be written in first-person point of view.

When writing personal narratives, you will usually be given a topic to write about. Here is an example.

> Think of a time when something exciting happened to you. Write a story about an exciting event that happened to you.

To write this story, think of one exciting event from your life. Be sure to choose just one event to write about. Then plan a story based on this event. You can list some ideas or take notes below.

Notes and Ideas

Use the table below to plan your story. Write or type a story of 1 to 2 pages.

The Beginning: Introduce the important features of your story. You might tell where and when the events take place and what you are doing.
→ Start your story by writing a paragraph that sets the scene.
The Middle: Describe the exciting event that happens.
→ Write two or three paragraphs that describe these events.
The Ending: Describe what happens in the end. You might tell how the event ended or how you felt at this time.
→ Write a paragraph that concludes your story.

Writing Prompt 66

Think of a time when you felt annoyed with someone. What made you feel annoyed? What did you do about how you felt?

Write a story about a time when you felt annoyed with someone. You can list some ideas or take notes below.

 Remember that you do not have to state how you felt. Instead, you can use details and descriptions to show how you felt.

Notes and Ideas

Use the table below to plan your story. Write or type a story of 1 to 2 pages.

The Beginning: Introduce the important features of your story. You might tell where and when the events take place and what you are doing.
→ **Start your story by writing a paragraph that sets the scene.**
The Middle: Describe what made you feel annoyed and what you did about it.
→ **Write two or three paragraphs that describe these events.**
The Ending: Describe what happens in the end. You might tell how the event ended or how you felt at this time.
→ **Write a paragraph that concludes your story.**

Writing Prompt 67

Think of a time when you learned how to do something new. Maybe you learned how to play the piano, how to do a card trick, or how to do karate.

Write a story about a time when you learned how to do something new. You can list some ideas or take notes below.

 Your story could be about one short event like a first piano lesson. It could also be about a longer series of events, such as how you practiced for years to become good at piano.

Notes and Ideas

Use the table below to plan your story. Write or type a story of 1 to 2 pages.

The Beginning: Introduce the important features of your story. You might tell where and when the events take place and what you are doing.
→ **Start your story by writing a paragraph that sets the scene.**
The Middle: Describe how you learned to do something new.
→ **Write two or three paragraphs that describe these events.**
The Ending: Describe what happens in the end. You might tell how the event ended or how you felt at this time.
→ **Write a paragraph that concludes your story.**

Writing Prompt 68

Think of a time when you tried to keep a secret from someone. Was it hard or easy to keep the secret? Did you keep the secret?

Write a story about a time when you tried to keep a secret from someone. You can list some ideas or take notes below.

Notes and Ideas

Use the table below to plan your story. Write or type a story of 1 to 2 pages.

The Beginning: Introduce the important features of your story. You might tell where and when the events take place and what you are doing.
→ Start your story by writing a paragraph that sets the scene.
The Middle: Describe how you tried to keep the secret.
→ Write two or three paragraphs that describe these events.
The Ending: Describe what happens in the end. You might tell how the event ended or how you felt at this time.
→ Write a paragraph that concludes your story.

Set 15: Write a Science Fiction Story

Writing Prompt 69

Science fiction stories are made-up stories that involve science in some way. Science fiction stories sometimes involve time travel.

Imagine that you are able to travel back in time. Think of a story about what happens when you travel back in time.

 Make your story about one problem that you have. Keep your story focused on solving that problem.

Use the table below to plan your story. Write or type a story of 1 to 2 pages.

The Beginning: Describe the main problem.
→ Start your story by writing a paragraph that introduces the problem.
The Middle: Describe how you try to solve the problem.
→ Write two or three paragraphs that describe these events.
The Ending: Describe how the problem is solved.
→End your story by writing a paragraph that shows that the problem is solved.

Writing Prompt 70

Write a story that begins with the sentences below.

> Craig looked around at the strange planet. He had never seen anything like it.

 Be sure not just to describe the planet. Instead, think of what happens to Craig on the strange planet.

Use the table below to plan your story. Write or type a story of 1 to 2 pages.

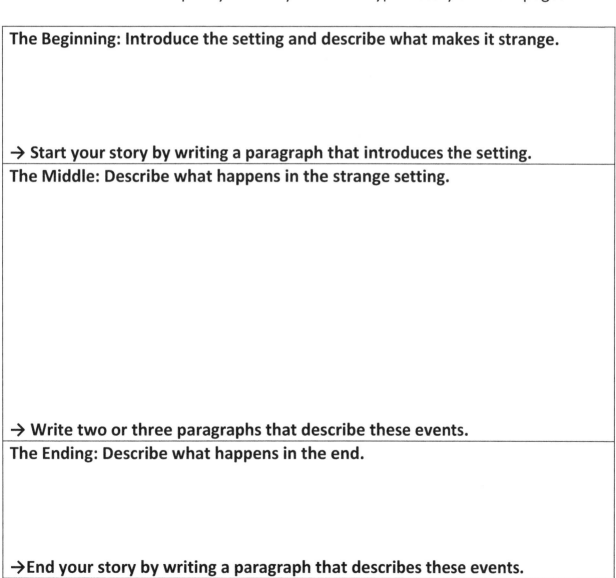

The Beginning: Introduce the setting and describe what makes it strange.

→ **Start your story by writing a paragraph that introduces the setting.**

The Middle: Describe what happens in the strange setting.

→ **Write two or three paragraphs that describe these events.**

The Ending: Describe what happens in the end.

→**End your story by writing a paragraph that describes these events.**

Writing Prompt 71

Emma was puzzled. There was a very strange object in her front yard. She had never seen anything like it. It looked like some kind of machine. Write a story about the object in Emma's front yard.

Use the table below to plan your story. Write or type a story of 1 to 2 pages.

The Beginning: Describe what happens first.
→ **Start your story by telling who the story is about and what is happening.**
The Middle: Describe what happens next.
→ **Continue the story by writing two or three paragraphs that describe what happens.**
The Ending: Describe what happens in the end.
→ **End your story by writing a paragraph that describes these events.**

Writing Prompt 72

Write a story about the problem described below.

A robot made to cook and clean stops doing what its master tells it to.

Use the table below to plan your story. Write or type a story of 1 to 2 pages.

The Beginning: Describe the main problem.
→ Start your story by writing a paragraph that introduces the problem.
The Middle: Describe what happens because of the problem.
→ Write two or three paragraphs that describe these events.
The Ending: Describe how the problem is solved.
→End your story by writing a paragraph that shows that the problem is solved.

Set 16: Write an Adventure Story

Writing Prompt 73

Adventure stories usually have exciting events. The characters often face dangers. Many adventure stories are set in the wild. The characters might have to cross a dangerous river, climb a mountain, or escape from a pack of wolves.

Imagine that you are on a field trip to the desert. Somehow, you get lost. It is getting dark and you are alone in the desert. Write a story about what happens.

Use the table below to plan your story. Write or type a story of 1 to 2 pages.

The Beginning: Introduce the setting and the main character.   **→ Start your story by writing a paragraph that tells where the story is set and what is happening.**
The Middle: Describe the exciting events that occur.   **→ Write two or three paragraphs that describe these events.**
The Ending: Describe what happens in the end.   **→End your story by writing a paragraph that describes these events.**

Writing Prompt 74

Sammy looked at the rushing river. He knew they could not swim across it. They would be washed away. They had to find another way across. Write a story about how Sammy crosses the river.

Use the table below to plan your story. Write or type a story of 1 to 2 pages.

The Beginning: Introduce the setting and the main character.   **→ Start your story by writing a paragraph that tells where the story is set and what is happening.**
The Middle: Describe the exciting events that occur.   **→ Write two or three paragraphs that describe these events.**
The Ending: Describe what happens in the end.   **→End your story by writing a paragraph that describes these events.**

Writing Prompt 75

Corey thought that the fishing trip sounded boring. He did not even want to go. But it turned out to be one of the most exciting days of his life. Write a story about the fishing trip and what made it exciting.

Use the table below to plan your story. Write or type a story of 1 to 2 pages.

The Beginning: Introduce the setting and the main character.
→ Start your story by writing a paragraph that tells where the story is set and what is happening.
The Middle: Describe the exciting events that occur.
→ Write two or three paragraphs that describe these events.
The Ending: Describe what happens in the end.
→End your story by writing a paragraph that describes these events.

Writing Prompt 76

Look at the picture below. Write an adventure story based on the picture.

Use the table below to plan your story. Write or type a story of 1 to 2 pages.

The Beginning: Introduce the setting and the main character.   **→ Start your story by writing a paragraph that tells where the story is set and what is happening.**
The Middle: Describe the exciting events that occur.   **→ Write two or three paragraphs that describe these events.**
The Ending: Describe what happens in the end.   **→End your story by writing a paragraph that describes these events.**

Set 17: Write a Diary Entry

Writing Prompt 77

Sometimes you will be asked to tell a story in the form of a diary entry. A diary entry is written in first-person point of view and can be less formal than a story. A good diary entry is focused on telling about one event. A good way to write a diary entry is to start by stating what happened, to give details about what happened in the middle, and then to end with your thoughts on what happened.

Now imagine that you met someone famous today. Write a diary entry describing what happened.

Use the table below to plan your writing. Write or type a diary entry of 1 to 2 pages.

The Beginning: Describe who you met and how you met the person.
→ Start your story by writing a paragraph that introduces the event.
The Middle: Describe what happened when you met the person.
→ Write two or three paragraphs that describe these events.
The Ending: Describe how you feel about what happened.
→ Write a paragraph that concludes your diary entry.

Writing Prompt 78

Imagine that you are a farmer. Write a diary entry describing an interesting event from your day.

 Your diary entry will be in first-person point of view. You will write it as if it is a farmer talking. You can choose language that a farmer might use to make it more interesting.

Use the table below to plan your writing. Write or type a diary entry of 1 to 2 pages.

The Beginning: Introduce the setting and the main character.
→ Start your diary entry by writing a paragraph that sets the scene.
The Middle: Describe the interesting event.
→ Write two or three paragraphs that describe the event.
The Ending: Describe how you feel about what happened.
→ Write a paragraph that concludes your diary entry.

Writing Prompt 79

Imagine that something very strange happened to you today. Write a diary entry describing what happened.

 You do not need to write about something that actually happened. Instead, make up a strange event but describe it as if it really happened.

Use the table below to plan your writing. Write or type a diary entry of 1 to 2 pages.

The Beginning: Introduce the setting and the main character.   → **Start your diary entry by writing a paragraph that sets the scene.**
The Middle: Describe the strange event.   → **Write two or three paragraphs that describe the event.**
The Ending: Describe how you feel about what happened.   → **Write a paragraph that concludes your diary entry.**

Writing Prompt 80

Write a diary entry that starts with the sentences below.

Dear Diary,

I really hate it when I fight with my sister. Today, Carla and I had a huge fight.

 The prompt tells you that the diary entry should be about a fight. You get to decide what the fight is about and what happens because of it.

Use the table below to plan your writing. Write or type a diary entry of 1 to 2 pages.

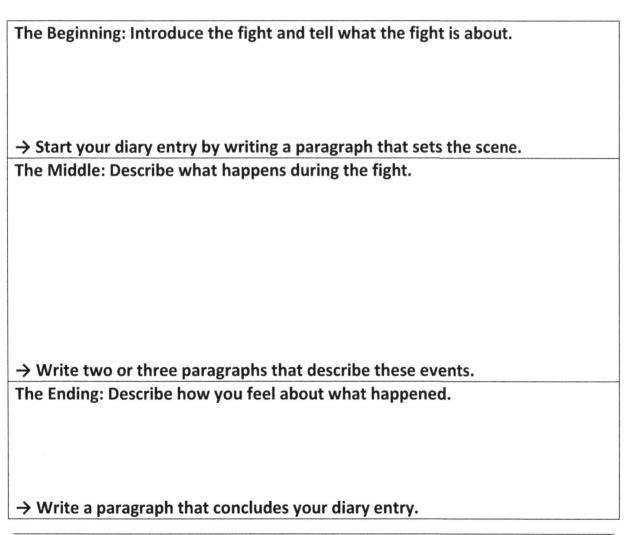

The Beginning: Introduce the fight and tell what the fight is about.
→ Start your diary entry by writing a paragraph that sets the scene.
The Middle: Describe what happens during the fight.
→ Write two or three paragraphs that describe these events.
The Ending: Describe how you feel about what happened.
→ Write a paragraph that concludes your diary entry.

Set 18: Write a Mystery Story

Writing Prompt 81

A mystery story is a story where there is a mystery or a puzzle to be solved. Most mystery stories have three parts.

The first part describes what the mystery is.
The second part describes how a character tries to solve the mystery.
The third part solves the mystery.

Use the table below to plan a mystery story about a missing shoe. Write or type a story of 1 to 2 pages.

The Case of the Missing Shoe

The Beginning: Describe the mystery.
→ Start your story by writing a paragraph that introduces the mystery.
The Middle: Describe how the main character tries to solve the mystery.
→ Write two or three paragraphs that describe these events.
The Ending: Describe how the mystery is solved.
→ Write a paragraph that concludes your story.

Writing Prompt 82

Write a mystery story with the title below.

The Ghost in the Picture Frame

 Mystery stories often have titles that describe the mystery. Use the title to come up with an idea for a story.

Use the table below to plan your story. Write or type a story of 1 to 2 pages.

The Beginning: Describe the mystery.
→ Start your story by writing a paragraph that introduces the mystery.
The Middle: Describe how the main character tries to solve the mystery.
→ Write two or three paragraphs that describe these events.
The Ending: Describe how the mystery is solved.
→ Write a paragraph that concludes your story.

Writing Prompt 83

Write a mystery story with the title below.

The Disappearing Dessert

Use the table below to plan your story. Write or type a story of 1 to 2 pages.

The Beginning: Describe the mystery.
→ Start your story by writing a paragraph that introduces the mystery.
The Middle: Describe how the main character tries to solve the mystery.
→ Write two or three paragraphs that describe these events.
The Ending: Describe how the mystery is solved.
→ Write a paragraph that concludes your story.

Writing Prompt 84

Write a mystery story with the title below.

The Stranger in the Stairwell

Use the table below to plan your story. Write or type a story of 1 to 2 pages.

The Beginning: Describe the mystery.   **→ Start your story by writing a paragraph that introduces the mystery.**
The Middle: Describe how the main character tries to solve the mystery.   **→ Write two or three paragraphs that describe these events.**
The Ending: Describe how the mystery is solved.   **→ Write a paragraph that concludes your story.**

Set 19: Write a Real-Life Story

Writing Prompt 85

A real-life story is any story that describes events that could really happen. Real-life stories often describe problems that real people face. Use the problem described below to write a story.

Sarah gets upset when her best friend makes a new friend.

Use the table below to plan your story. Write or type a story of 1 to 2 pages.

The Beginning: Describe who the character is and what the main problem is.   → **Start by writing a paragraph that introduces the character's problem.**
The Middle: Describe how the main character tries to solve the problem.   → **Write two or three paragraphs that describe these events.**
The Ending: Describe what happens in the end to solve the problem.   →**End your story by writing a paragraph that shows that the problem is solved.**

Writing Prompt 86

Kennedy is walking to school when he sees a man grab a woman's bag and run off. Kennedy decides to chase the man. Write a story about what happens next.

Use the table below to plan your story. Write or type a story of 1 to 2 pages.

The Beginning: Describe who the character is and what the main problem is.
→ Start by writing a paragraph that introduces the character's problem.
The Middle: Describe how the main character tries to solve the problem.
→ Write two or three paragraphs that describe these events.
The Ending: Describe what happens in the end to solve the problem.
→End your story by writing a paragraph that shows that the problem is solved.

Writing Prompt 87

Josh checked his hiking pack and decided he had everything he needed. He had no idea that something was missing. Write a story about what Josh is missing.

 Start the story at the point when Josh first realizes that he is missing something. Use the rest of the story to describe what he does about it.

Use the table below to plan your story. Write or type a story of 1 to 2 pages.

The Beginning: Describe who the character is and what the main problem is.   **→ Start by writing a paragraph that introduces the character's problem.**
The Middle: Describe how the main character tries to solve the problem.   **→ Write two or three paragraphs that describe these events.**
The Ending: Describe what happens in the end to solve the problem.   **→End your story by writing a paragraph that shows that the problem is solved.**

Writing Prompt 88

Victor stepped up onto the stage. He was about to take part in the spelling bee. Suddenly, he felt very nervous. He feared he would forget how to spell even a simple word. Write a story about how Victor does in the spelling bee.

Use the table below to plan your story. Write or type a story of 1 to 2 pages.

The Beginning: Describe who the character is and what the main problem is.   → **Start by writing a paragraph that introduces the character's problem.**
The Middle: Describe how the main character tries to solve the problem.   → **Write two or three paragraphs that describe these events.**
The Ending: Describe what happens in the end to solve the problem.   →**End your story by writing a paragraph that shows that the problem is solved.**

Set 20: Write an Animal Story

Writing Prompt 89

Animal stories use animals as characters, but the animals act more like people. The animals think, feel, and usually talk. Write a story based on the idea below.

A zebra is jealous of a leopard's spots.

Use the table below to plan your story. Write or type a story of 1 to 2 pages.

The Beginning: Describe who the character is and what the main problem is.   → **Start by writing a paragraph that introduces the character's problem.**
The Middle: Describe how the main character tries to solve the problem.   → **Write two or three paragraphs that describe these events.**
The Ending: Describe what happens in the end to solve the problem.   →**End your story by writing a paragraph that shows that the problem is solved.**

Writing Prompt 90

Write a story from the point of view of a frog. Think about what problem the frog could have.

Use the table below to plan your story. Write or type a story of 1 to 2 pages.

The Beginning: Describe who the character is and what the main problem is.
→ Start by writing a paragraph that introduces the character's problem.
The Middle: Describe how the main character tries to solve the problem.
→ Write two or three paragraphs that describe these events.
The Ending: Describe what happens in the end to solve the problem.
→End your story by writing a paragraph that shows that the problem is solved.

Writing Prompt 91

Write a story about two animals who become unlikely friends.

Use the table below to plan your story. Write or type a story of 1 to 2 pages.

The Beginning: Introduce the two characters who will become friends.
→ Start your story by writing a paragraph that introduces the characters.
The Middle: Describe how the two characters become friends.
→ Write two or three paragraphs that describe these events.
The Ending: Describe what happens in the end.
→End your story by writing a paragraph that concludes your story.

Writing Prompt 92

Look at the picture below. Write a story about the character shown.

Use the table below to plan your story. Write or type a story of 1 to 2 pages.

The Beginning: Describe who the character is and what the main problem is.
→ Start by writing a paragraph that introduces the character's problem.
The Middle: Describe how the main character tries to solve the problem.
→ Write two or three paragraphs that describe these events.
The Ending: Describe what happens in the end to solve the problem.
→End your story by writing a paragraph that shows that the problem is solved.

Set 21: Write from a Title

Writing Prompt 93

The title of a story can tell what the story is mainly about. Write a story with the title below.

The Scariest Pet of All

Use the table below to plan your story. Write or type a story of 1 to 2 pages.

The Beginning: Describe what happens first.
→ Start your story by telling who the story is about and what is happening.
The Middle: Describe what happens next.
→ Write two or three paragraphs that describe these events.
The Ending: Describe what happens in the end.
→End your story by writing a paragraph that concludes your story.

Writing Prompt 94

The title of a story can describe the main problem of a story. Write a story with the title below.

The Day Leticia Got Locked in the Library

Use the table below to plan your story. Write or type a story of 1 to 2 pages.

The Beginning: Describe the main problem.
→ Start your story by writing a paragraph that introduces the problem.
The Middle: Describe how the main character tries to solve the problem.
→ Write two or three paragraphs that describe these events.
The Ending: Describe how the problem is solved.
→End your story by writing a paragraph that shows that the problem is solved.

Writing Prompt 95

The title of a story can describe how a character in the story changes. Write a story with the title below.

How Conrad Learned to Forgive

Use the table below to plan your story. Write or type a story of 1 to 2 pages.

The Beginning: Introduce the main character.   **→ Start your story by writing a paragraph that describes who the main character is and what the main character is like.**
The Middle: Describe what happens to change the main character.   **→ Write two or three paragraphs that describe these events.**
The Ending: Describe how the main character changes.   **→Write a paragraph that shows that the main character has changed.**

Writing Prompt 96

The title of a story can describe the main theme of a story. Write a story with the title below.

Practice Makes Perfect

 Think of how a character might learn that practice makes perfect. Then use these events as the plot of your story.

Use the table below to plan your story. Write or type a story of 1 to 2 pages.

The Beginning: Introduce the main character and show what he or she is like.   **→ Start your story by showing what the main character is like and what is happening.**
The Middle: Describe what happens to teach the character a lesson.   **→ Write two or three paragraphs that describe these events.**
The Ending: Describe how the character has learned a lesson.   **→ Write a paragraph that shows how the character has changed.**

Set 22: Write a Letter

Writing Prompt 97

Some stories are told in the form of letters. Just like stories, the events are made up. However, you write them in first-person point of view as if you are writing to tell someone about the events. One good way to write a story in the form of a letter is described below.

> The beginning introduces the topic or states what the letter is about.
> The middle gives details about the topic or describes the events.
> The ending sums up what happened or shows how the character feels.

 Letters are less formal than many stories. You can write letters as if you are writing to a friend or family member to tell them something.

The table below shows a plan for a letter. Use the plan to write a letter. Write or type a letter of 1 to 2 pages.

The Beginning: Introduce the topic of the letter.

I went on a class trip to the museum and things went wrong.

→ Start your letter by writing a paragraph that tells what the letter is about.

The Middle: Describe the main events.

We were in a room full of statues. My friend Jack pushed me. I knocked over a statue. It smashed on the floor. I got in a lot of trouble. Jack didn't get in trouble at all.

→ Write two or three paragraphs that describe these events.

The Ending: Summarize what happened or show how the character feels.

I am never going back to the museum again. I am never talking to Jack again.

→End your letter by writing a paragraph that sums up the events.

Writing Prompt 98

Write a letter that describes how a character lost something that was very special.

Use the table below to plan your letter. Write or type a letter of 1 to 2 pages.

The Beginning: Introduce the topic of the letter.   **→ Start your letter by writing a paragraph that tells what the letter is about.**
The Middle: Describe the main events.   **→ Write two or three paragraphs that describe these events.**
The Ending: Summarize what happened or show how the character feels.   **→End your letter by writing a paragraph that sums up the events.**

Writing Prompt 99

Write a letter that describes how a character dressed up as a clown for a children's birthday party.

Use the table below to plan your letter. Write or type a letter of 1 to 2 pages.

The Beginning: Introduce the topic of the letter.   → **Start your letter by writing a paragraph that tells what the letter is about.**
The Middle: Describe the main events.   → **Write two or three paragraphs that describe these events.**
The Ending: Summarize what happened or show how the character feels.   →**End your letter by writing a paragraph that sums up the events.**

Writing Prompt 100

Letters can also be about true events. You can write about events from your own life. Write a letter that describes something interesting that happened to you this week. The interesting event will be the topic of your letter.

Use the table below to plan your letter. Write or type a letter of 1 to 2 pages.

The Beginning: Introduce the topic of the letter.
→ **Start your letter by writing a paragraph that tells what the letter is about.**
The Middle: Describe the main events.
→ **Write two or three paragraphs that describe these events.**
The Ending: Summarize what happened or show how you feel.
→**End your letter by writing a paragraph that sums up the events.**

WRITING REVIEW AND SCORING GUIDE
For Parents, Teachers, and Tutors

Each set of writing prompts is designed to help students focus on one aspect of narrative writing or one genre of narrative writing. The scoring guides below list key factors that should be considered when reviewing writing tasks in each set.

After students have completed each writing task, review their work based on the factors listed. Identify strengths, weaknesses, and changes that can be made to improve their work. Give students guidance on what to focus on in the next writing task to improve their score.

Developing Writing Skills

Set 1: Describing Events in Order

Review the student's work based on the following key factors.
- Is there a clear sequence of events?
- Does the paragraph have a beginning, a middle, and an ending?
- Are the events described in order?

Warm-Up Exercise: Relating Events to Each Other

Each box should be completed with an event that would cause the last event. Any event can be accepted as long as it links the first and last event to show a complete plot.
Possible answers from top to bottom:
A huge fish is caught that weighs down the whole boat.
Steven crashes his bike on the way to school.
They paint the room purple and green, but it looks awful.
Abby writes a letter to her local newspaper.
Gia tells everyone the secret.

Set 2: Understanding Plot

Review the student's work based on the following key factors.
- Is there a clear sequence of events?
- Does the story have a beginning, a middle, and an ending?
- Are the events described in order?
- Is the story focused on one set of events?
- Does the story have a clear ending?

Warm-Up Exercise: Problems and Solutions

The student should list three more ways that each problem could be solved. Any solution can be accepted as long as it relates to the problem.

Note: Stories can describe events that could not really occur in real life. Students may need to be encouraged to use their imaginations to think of interesting or creative ways the problem could be solved.

Set 3: Using a Main Problem

Review the student's work based on the following key factors.
- Does the start of the story describe a main problem?
- Does the middle of the story describe how the problem is solved?
- Does the ending of the story include some sort of resolution?
- Are there clear transitions between events in the story?

Warm-Up Exercise: Introducing the Setting

The student should write one or two sentences that help show what the setting is without actually stating it. Any answer can be accepted as long as it includes at least one detail that helps reveal the setting.

Set 4: Understanding Setting

Review the student's work based on the following key factors.
- Is the correct setting used?
- Is the story focused on a set of events taking place in the setting?
- Does the story have a beginning, a middle, and an ending?

Note: A common mistake made when writing based on setting is to focus too much on describing the setting. The setting should be thought of as the starting point for a story. It should be used to come up with an idea for events that occur in that setting.

Warm-Up Exercise: Characters and Traits

The student should complete the table with an action that someone with the trait might do or a detail that shows that someone has the trait. Any answer can be accepted as long as the action or detail relates to the trait.

Set 5: Creating a Main Character

Review the student's work based on the following key factors.
- Is there one clear main character?
- Are the character's personality traits clearly shown?
- Does a series of events occur based on what the character is like?
- Does the end of the story include some sort of resolution?

Note: The resolution of the story can be that the character solves a problem, that the character changes, or that the character learns a lesson.

Warm-Up Exercise: Choosing Action Words

The student should complete each question by replacing the underlined verb with a stronger verb. Strong answers will choose a verb that relates to the event described in the sentence and suggests how something was done. Possible answers are given below.
1. chatted   2. jammed   3. sprang   4. smashed   5. grinned   6. peeped

Set 6: Describing Actions

Review the student's work based on the following key factors.
- Do the actions listed fit with the purpose described?
- Does the paragraph describe actions effectively?
- Does the paragraph show by using actions instead of telling?

Warm-Up Exercise: Using Feelings in Stories

The student should complete the table with a feeling to match each event or an event to match each feeling. Any feeling or event is acceptable as long as there is a reasonable link between the event and how it would make someone feel. Possible answers from top to bottom: scared; annoyed; proud; cheerful; being stuck inside on a rainy day; winning a prize; tripping over in front of everyone; learning a big storm is coming; seeing your bike is not where you left it.

Set 7: Using Descriptions to Show Feelings

Review the student's work based on the following key factors.
- Are descriptions used to show what characters are like?
- Are descriptions used to show how characters feel?
- Are the descriptions effective at showing how characters feel?
- Does the story have a beginning, a middle, and an ending?
- Does the character change during the story?

Warm-Up Exercise: Using Punctuation in Dialogue

The student should complete each question by placing the quotation marks in the correct place. Answers are given below.
1. George said, "I am feeling sick today."
2. "Is everything all right?" Carol asked.
3. "I liked the camp," Mark said. "I would like to go again."
4. "Watch out!" Jenna yelled.
5. Sandy asked, "Can I wash the dishes up later?"
6. "The party was great," Hannah said. "Why didn't you come?"
7. "We should plan something fun to do on the weekend," Kyle said.

Set 8: Using Dialogue

Review the student's work based on the following key factors.
- Does the student include dialogue in the story?
- Is the dialogue effective at showing what is happening?
- Is the dialogue effective at showing how characters feel?
- Does the dialogue blend well with the rest of the story?
- Does the dialogue sound like how people really speak?

Note: Some students make the mistake of trying to write a whole story in dialogue. The key to using dialogue is to use it as a technique within a story.

Set 9: Understanding Theme

Review the student's work based on the following key factors.
- Does the story have a clear theme or a clear message?
- Are the events of the story based on a theme?
- Is there a clear sequence of events?
- Does the story have a beginning, a middle, and an ending?
- Can the reader understand the theme without it being stated?

Note: When writing based on a theme, some students make the mistake of writing an essay instead of a story. Students write about their opinion on the theme. You may need to remind students that they need to think of a story idea based on the theme. The story idea will involve a set of events that teach the lesson or communicate the theme.

Warm-Up Exercise: Writing in First-Person

The student should rewrite each sentence in first-person point of view by replacing the underlined words. Answers are given below.
1. I walked into the room and took my seat.
2. I placed my bag on the ground.
3. I was mad at my team because I knew we should have won.
4. I saw that the last name on the list was mine.
5. I was sad that nobody asked me how I was feeling.
6. I asked my sister to help me clean our room.

Set 10: Using a Narrator

Review the student's work based on the following key factors.
- Is the story written in first-person point of view?
- Does the story show the narrator's feelings?
- Do the narrator's feelings change throughout the story?
- Does the narrator's voice suit the character?

Note: Voice refers to how the character sounds. A story with a young narrator will have a different voice than one with an older narrator. You may suggest that students think about how the character would sound if you were speaking to him or her. Then encourage students to write the story in the voice of the character.

Warm-Up Exercise: Using Transition Words

The student should write two sentences each using examples of words and phrases telling when events occur, the order of events, and how much time passed. Any sentence can be accepted as long as it uses the word or phrase in a reasonable way. Sample answers are given below.
When Events Occur
1. I saw something strange outside this morning.
2. Joy snuck out of her room late at night.
Order of Events
1. After school, I went to my dance class.
2. Haley finished the test right before the bell rang.
How Much Time Passed
1. After a short time, I packed up the picnic.
2. The day after first meeting Yuri, Craig saw him again.

Set 11: Understanding Sequence

Review the student's work based on the following key factors.
- Is there a clear sequence of events?
- Does the story have a beginning, a middle, and an ending?
- Are transition words and phrases used to tell when events take place, and to transition between events?
- Are transition words and phrases used to show how much time has passed?
- Are the transition words and phrases used appropriate and effective?

Set 12: Using Humor

Review the student's work based on the following key factors.
- Does the story include humor?
- Are humorous events clearly described?
- Does the story include details and descriptions?
- Is there a clear sequence of events?
- Does the story have a beginning, a middle, and an ending?

Applying Writing Skills

Set 13: Write from a Picture Prompt

Review the student's work based on the following key factors.
- Is the story idea based on the picture?
- Is the story focused on one set of events?
- Does the story have a beginning, a middle, and an ending?
- Is the story well-organized with clear transitions?
- Are details and descriptions used effectively?
- Are strong and effective word choices used?
- Are there no or few errors in grammar and usage?

Note: Some students make the mistake of writing a description of what the picture shows. You may need to remind students to use the picture to come up with an idea for a story.

Set 14: Write a Personal Narrative

Review the student's work based on the following key factors.
- Is the story written in first-person point of view?
- Is the story focused on one set of events?
- Does the story have a beginning, a middle, and an ending?
- Is the story well-organized with clear transitions?
- Are the events clearly described?
- Is there some sort of resolution?
- Are details and descriptions used effectively?
- Are strong and effective word choices used?
- Are there no or few errors in grammar and usage?

Set 15: Write a Science Fiction Story

Review the student's work based on the following key factors.
- Is the story based on one well-developed idea?
- Does the story have a beginning, a middle, and an ending?
- Is the story well-organized with clear transitions?
- Is there some sort of resolution?
- Are details and descriptions used effectively?
- Are strong and effective word choices used?
- Are there no or few errors in grammar and usage?

Set 16: Write an Adventure Story

Review the student's work based on the following key factors.
- Is the setting established well?
- Does the story have a beginning, a middle, and an ending?
- Is the story well-organized with clear transitions?
- Is there some sort of resolution?
- Are details and descriptions used effectively?
- Are strong and effective word choices used?
- Are the events described in a way that makes them seem exciting?
- Are there no or few errors in grammar and usage?

Note: Adventure stories are a good opportunity for students to practice using descriptions. Descriptions can be used to help show how great the problems are. For example, descriptions could be used in the first story to show how dark and scary the desert is, or used in the second story to show how fast-moving and dangerous the river is.

Set 17: Write a Diary Entry

Review the student's work based on the following key factors.
- Are the ideas well-developed?
- Is the diary entry focused?
- Is there a clear sequence of events?
- Does the diary entry have a beginning, a middle, and an ending?
- Does the diary entry include details and descriptions?
- Is there some sort of resolution?
- Are there no or few errors in grammar and usage?

Note: Diary entries are a good opportunity for students to develop a voice. Remind students that a diary entry does not have to be formal. They can write it in a casual way. They can also write it how they imagine the character would speak.

Set 18: Write a Mystery Story

Review the student's work based on the following key factors.
- Is the story based on one well-developed idea?
- Does the story have a beginning, a middle, and an ending?
- Is the story well-organized with clear transitions?
- Is there a resolution where the mystery is solved?
- Are details and descriptions used effectively?
- Are strong and effective word choices used?
- Are there no or few errors in grammar and usage?

Set 19: Write a Real-Life Story

Review the student's work based on the following key factors.
- Is the character and the character's problem established well?
- Is the story well-organized with clear transitions?
- Is the story focused on a character solving a problem?
- Is there some sort of resolution?
- Are details and descriptions used effectively?
- Are strong and effective word choices used?
- Are there no or few errors in grammar and usage?

Set 20: Write an Animal Story

Review the student's work based on the following key factors.
- Are the ideas well-developed?
- Are the characters well-developed?
- Does the story have a beginning, a middle, and an ending?
- Is the story well-organized with clear transitions?
- Is there some sort of resolution?
- Are details and descriptions used effectively?
- Are strong and effective word choices used?
- Are there no or few errors in grammar and usage?

Set 21: Write from a Title

Review the student's work based on the following key factors.
- Is the story idea based on the title?
- Is the story focused on one set of events?
- Does the story have a beginning, a middle, and an ending?
- Is the story well-organized with clear transitions?
- Are the events clearly described?
- Is there some sort of resolution?
- Are details and descriptions used effectively?
- Are strong and effective word choices used?
- Are there no or few errors in grammar and usage?

Set 22: Write a Letter

Review the student's work based on the following key factors.
- Is the letter written in first-person point of view?
- Is the letter focused on one set of events?
- Does the letter have a beginning, a middle, and an ending?
- Is the letter well-organized with clear transitions?
- Are the events clearly described?
- Does the letter show how the narrator feels?
- Does the letter end with an effective summary or resolution?
- Are details and descriptions used effectively?
- Are strong and effective word choices used?
- Are there no or few errors in grammar and usage?

COMMON CORE STATE STANDARDS
For Parents, Teachers, and Tutors

The Common Core State Standards are a set of standards that have been adopted by most American states. The standards describe what students are expected to be able to do. Student learning is based on these standards throughout the year.

The Common Core writing standards divide writing skills based on text type and purpose. One of the text types covered is narrative writing, which is writing designed mainly to entertain. This book focuses specifically on narrative writing.

This workbook provides full coverage of the narrative writing skills that Grade 3 students are expected to have. The exercises and writing tasks, guidance given, and review and scoring guide have been specifically developed based on the skills listed in the Common Core State Standards. The full content of this standard is given below.

Students will often be assessed in class based on these standards and they act as a guideline for how narrative writing tasks are scored and what skills are expected to be seen in narrative texts that students produce. Depending on state, students may also be assessed on a state test that includes a writing prompt where students produce narrative writing.

Common Core Narrative Writing Standard for Grade 3

Write narratives to develop real or imagined experiences or events using effective technique, descriptive details, and clear event sequences.

a. Establish a situation and introduce a narrator and/or characters; organize an event sequence that unfolds naturally.

b. Use dialogue and descriptions of actions, thoughts, and feelings to develop experiences and events or show the response of characters to situations.

c. Use temporal words and phrases to signal event order.

d. Provide a sense of closure.

Take writing skills to the next level with the Common Core Language series.

Designed to enhance language and vocabulary skills to exceed grade level expectations, the four books in the language series complement this writing workbook. They will provide students with the language and vocabulary skills they need to produce high-quality writing that demonstrates advanced ability.

Made in the USA
Columbia, SC
27 June 2025